ROCKY MOUNTAIN WILDLIFE

David Hancock

Photos: **Brian Wolitski**
David Hancock

hancock
house

ISBN 0-88839-567-1

Printed in Indonesia—T K PRINTING
Production: Rick Groenheyde, Laura Michaels

Cataloging in Publication Data

Hancock, David, 1938-
    Rocky Mountain Wildlife / David Hancock ; photos, Brian Wolitski,
David Hancock.

ISBN 0-88839-567-1

    1. Mammals--Rocky Mountains. I. Wolitski, Brian, 1958- II. Title.

QL721.5.R83H35 2005   599'.0978   C2005-901354-0

Published simultaneously in Canada and the United States by

HANCOCK HOUSE PUBLISHERS LTD.
19313 Zero Avenue, Surrey, B.C. V3S 9R9
(604) 538-1114 Fax (604) 538-2262

HANCOCK HOUSE PUBLISHERS
1431 Harrison Avenue, Blaine, WA 98230-5005
(604) 538-1114 Fax (604) 538-2262

Website: www.hancockhouse.com *Email:* sales@hancockhouse.com

Contents

FOREWORD

The northern Rocky Mountains described in this book extend over a vast area from British Columbia's Peace River down to the Colorado–New Mexico border in the south. Providing scientists and amateur naturalists alike with immense diversity in landform, climate, and vegetation, the area abounds with a wide variety of wildlife and birds.

Rocky Mountain Wildlife is primarily a reference work intended for readers requiring a compact, easy-to-read compendium of information on the area's ecology, its spectacular mammals, their habitats, social organization, distribution, and migratory patterns.

The photographs are the selection of two seasoned field photographers: biologist David Hancock and Brian Wolitski — one of the Rockies' most experienced and consummate picture takers.

The natural history folios give a succinct textual summary and an extensive visual representation of each major species of Rocky Mountain mammals. The emphasis here is to show the life habits through photography. Deep appreciation is extended to biologist Don Blood for reviewing this selection of the mountain wildlife he so intimately knows.

INTRODUCTION

What and Where

The Rocky Mountains have had a profound, humbling influence on many people from the earliest explorers and mountain men to modern tourists. The Rockies are without doubt a striking segment of the vast North American landscape. Their distant peaks once fired the imaginations of Anthony Henday, Lewis and Clark, and John Palliser; then seemed to be barely surmountable barriers to transcontinental railroads and highways, and have finally emerged as a soul restoring retreat for millions of harassed city dwellers.

Partly because so many North Americans seek out mountainous places for relaxation and enjoyment, and see them as their special places, it seems worthwhile to present a factual, illustrated account of the wild mammals and birds likely to be encountered there. Certainly the opportunity to see wildlife in a natural setting is a strong attraction for the Rocky Mountain visitors, be they family campers, keen naturalists, or hikers and outdoor enthusiasts.

While the term "Rocky Mountains" conjures up an instant picture in the minds of nearly everyone, the geographical extent of the Rocky Mountain region is not easy to define. Generally speaking this up and down land mass extends from the Yukon and Northwest Territories to Mexico. The eastern side of the Rocky Mountain chain, where the Great Plains roll like a blanket to their very foot, is quite well defined. Usually a narrow band of foothills and occasionally an outlier of low mountains in the adjacent plains is all that separates these two great regions.

To the west, however, a complex array of north-south ranges and associated intermountain basins and plateaus extend to the Pacific shores. This whole area, known as a cordillera, has a certain uniformity of wildlife due to its terrain.

But of all our western mountains, the Rockies are best known and best loved. They are renowned for the scenic splendor of places like Banff, Glacier, and Yellowstone National Parks. Our discussion of the wildlife of this spectacular region includes typical species found in the main chain of the Rockies from areas around the Peace River in British Columbia to the Colorado–New Mexico border. Included are the more prominent foothills along the eastern side, and those main ranges to the west which lie between the Interior Plateau, Great Basin region and the Rockies proper. For the purposes of this book, the "Rockies" includes the Caribou, Purcell and Selkirk Ranges in British Columbia, the Clearwater and Salmon River Ranges in Idaho, Uinta Mountains of northeastern Utah, and virtually all the mountains of Alberta, Montana, Wyoming, and Colorado.

Incomparable Diversity

The great drawing card of mountains in general and the Rockies in particular is their immense diversity in landforms and living things. No other physiographic region of North America compares with its variety of wildlife. Let's take a look at the reasons for this.

In the first place, the fauna is heterogenous because a wide variety of habitat is available; the habitats are many because of the landscape diversity. The physical stage on which the native plants and animals exist is raised and twisted so that elevations, steepness, and the directions which slopes face, are each unique. Superimposed on this contorted landscape are additional diversifying factors, such as varying or absent soil, watercourses, temperature and wind, plus unpredictable snow avalanches.

Compare this region with other landscapes of North America. The extensive Great Plains, in its pristine state, was an ocean of grass interrupted only occasionally by badlands, sandhills, or river valleys. One could walk for miles in the same kind of habitat. The vast boreal forest presents mile after mile of spruce forest broken occasionally by lakes, muskeg, and fire scars, but has little physical or climactic diversity. Likewise the Arctic Tundra displays little variance. Each of these huge areas of relatively consistent geography thus provide many fewer niches for wild birds and mammals to occupy. Yet there are few places in the mountains where the hiker can proceed for more than a mile or two without passing through varying countryside.

Elevation chiefly affects wildlife habitat through variations in weather and climate. Within the region, elevations vary from about 3,000 to 13,000 feet above sea level, and climate ranges from almost desert-like in the southern valleys to arctic-alpine near the peaks. Mountain soils, mostly derived from broken rock, also differ with elevation. They tend to be well developed in the broad, lower valleys, less developed on the middle elevation forest slopes, and little more than pulverized rock or boulders on the higher peaks. Therefore, severe climate and poor soils restrict growth of plants and productivity of wildlife habitat at higher elevations.

Anyone who labors up a mountain trail will recognize that slopes change in steepness, as well as orientation. Orientation, the direction the slopes face, is described as "aspect," and both steepness and aspect affect local climate and the resulting array of plants and wildlife. In valleys running east and west,

in particular, the mountain traveller may notice one side of the valley has vastly different growth than the other. In the Rocky Mountain region, southerly exposed slopes are usually quite open and covered with a scattering of trees, scrub, or even grassland, while the northerly aspect has dense forest growth. This is because the slope facing north receives little or no direct sunlight, remains cool and loses little moisture by evaporation. The opposite is true of the side which faces the sun. Because birds and mammals depend upon vegetation for most of their requirements, they are also affected by slope steepness, so that quite different aggregations of wildlife can be expected to occupy the two sides of such a valley.

Broad climatic patterns also effect the distribution of vegetation and wildlife in the Rockies. While local factors of elevation, steepness, and aspect already mentioned contribute to diversity on any one mountain, so do gradual differences in climate from north to south and east to west across the region. Since this region extends about 1,600 miles from south to north, climate at any one elevation becomes progressively severe as one proceeds northward, and as a result plants and animals take on more northern affinities.

Climate varies considerably from the western to eastern slopes of the Rockies due to the "rain shadow" effect. These mountains exert a powerful influence on the moisture-laden air masses, which move inland from the Pacific, deflecting them upward so that they drop most of their moisture on the western and windward side, spoiling many a mountain camping trip. The winds then push the now dryer and lighter air masses over the mountain where the eastern leeward slopes receive much less precipitation. As a result, rapid changes in rainfall and, therefore, in vegetation occur over quite short distances in the Rockies; and denser forest with more luxuriant undergrowth occurs on the western slope.

Although the rain shadow effect is most pronounced in the coastal ranges—the first to be buffeted by Pacific storms—it is still noticeable in the Rockies. One of the best examples of the east slope versus west slope characteristics, as well as of elevational change, can be experienced by driving along the Going-to-the-Sun-Road, a highway which completely traverses Glacier National Park, Montana.

Altitudinal Changes in Vegetational Zones

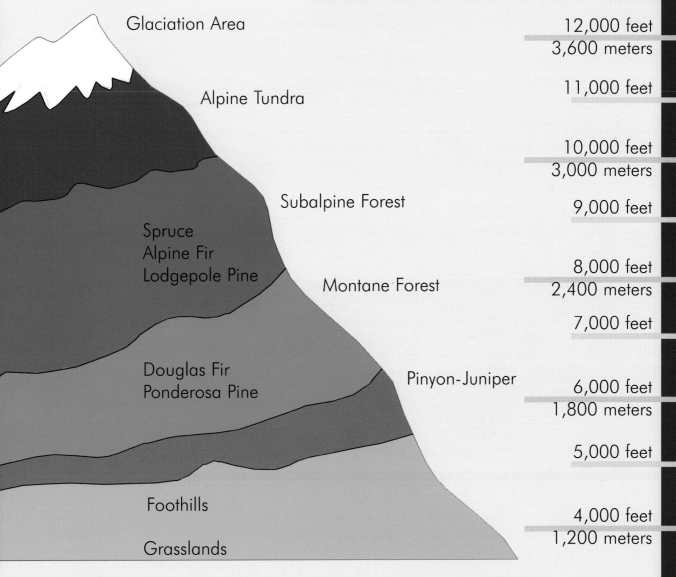

Glaciation Area — 12,000 feet / 3,600 meters

Alpine Tundra — 11,000 feet

Subalpine Forest — 10,000 feet / 3,000 meters — 9,000 feet

Spruce
Alpine Fir
Lodgepole Pine

Montane Forest — 8,000 feet / 2,400 meters — 7,000 feet

Douglas Fir
Ponderosa Pine

Pinyon-Juniper — 6,000 feet / 1,800 meters — 5,000 feet

Foothills — 4,000 feet / 1,200 meters

Grasslands

Mountain Sheep
Ovis canadensis

Vital Statistics:

	Ram	Ewe
Horned sex	Both	
Birth weight	10-14 lbs.	
Adult weight	150-275 lb.	125-200 lb.
Adult shoulder height	37-41"	32-36"
Maximum lifespan	19 yrs.	24 yrs.

Ram Horns:

Age	Points (one side)	Max. Length	Max. Weight
1½	1		
2½	3-4		
3½	4-6		
4+	6-8	62 ins.	25-35 lbs.

Reproduction:

Rams: Can breed at 2-3 years, but most mating is by older rams. Rutting season is November-December.

Ewes: Produce first lamb at 3 to 4 years. Gestation period six months.

Lambs: One per birth usual; twins rare. Birth season May-June.

Food:

Grasses and grass-like plants are important at all seasons. Important species include wheatgrasses, fescue, and needlegrass. Other favorite foods include pasture sage, dwarf alpine willow, and lupines.

Habitat:

Bighorn sheep inhabit alpine meadows and grassy mountain slopes in proximity to rugged rocky cliffs during summer. During winter they come down to lower grassy benches and wind blown slopes.

Bighorn ram in pursuit of a ewe during rut season.

Bighorn rams making close eye contact.

Bighorn sheep are grazers and enjoy the lush grasses and forests along the roadside.

Ram "lip curl" is a sign he is testing the air to determine a ewe's receptivity to breeding.

This young ram is molting during the summer and will have a new warm coat for winter.

Bighorn rams guard ewe during breeding season.

Mountain Goat

Oreamnos americanus

Vital Statistics:

	Billy	Nanny
Horned sex	Billy and nanny	
Birth weight	About 7 lbs.	
Adult weight	140-250 lbs.	100-210 lbs.
Adult shoulder height	40-44 in.	35-40 in.
Maximum lifespan	Not known	

Horns:

Male horns thicker at base and curve gradually near the tip. Nanny horns curve sharply at tip. Record horn length 12 in., but average about 9 in. for billies and 8 in. for nannies.

Reproduction:

Billies: Sexually mature at 1½ to 2½ years of age, but most breeding is by older males. Rutting period about November.

Nannies: Produce first young at about 3 years of age. Gestation period about 180 days.

Kids: One is usual, but up to 25 percent of births may be twins. Young born May-June.

Food:

Very variable food habits. Grasses, sedges, and herbs important in spring and summer, including kobresia, bluegrasses, wheatgrass, fescue, and clover. Woody browse eaten in winter includes willows, bear-berry, blueberries, Douglas fir, and alpine fir.

Habitat:

Mountain goats inhabit the most rugged mountain terrain, frequenting in winter cliffs too sheer to hold snow. They also forage alpine meadows and forests—all the way to sea level along the British Columbia coast.

A nanny and young kid enjoy new spring grasses along roadside.

Mountain goats enjoy the rugged alpine zone but they do frequently descend to the river valleys and mineral licks to obtain salts.

A mountain goat at home in the rugged high alpine of the rockies.

Mountain goat in early summer shedding winter fur.

In summer and fall, a new warm coat grows in to provide winter warmth.

Mountain Goats are remarkably sure-footed and will climb steep rocky cliffs predators will not attempt.

Goats both graze grasses and browse subalpine stunted tree shoots.

Bison or Buffalo

Bison bison

Vital Statistics:

	Bull	Cow
Horned sex	Bull and cow	
Birth weight	No information	
Adult weight	900-1800 lbs.	750-1100 lbs.
Adult shoulder height	60-72 in.	52-60 in.
Maximum lifespan	Up to 40 years	

Horns:

Horns project laterally in the calves, then gradually turn upward, and finally inward at the tips in adult animals. Male horns larger than those of female.

Reproduction:

Bulls: Most reach sexual maturity at 2-3 years of age. Rutting period is July to September.

Cows: A few precocious cows conceive as yearlings. About half of the two-year-olds conceive (bear first young at about third birthday). All females sexually mature by 3½ years of age, but usually only produce about 2 calves every 3 years. Gestation period 270-300 days.

Calves: One is the rule. Mostly born from late April into June.

Food:

Grasses, sedges, and small herbs predominate. Staple foods include wheatgrasses, fescue, bluegrass, and brome.

Habitat:

The buffalo, now exterminated from the prairies, occupies aspen parkland, grassy benches and open coniferous forests.

It is estimated that during the century before Europeans explored North America, some 60 million bison roamed the continent.

Today remnant populations of plains buffalo can be seen throughout the Rocky Mountains and adjacent plains, parks, and ranches.

Wapiti or Elk

Cervus elaphus

Vital Statistics:

	Bull	Cow
Antlered sex	Bull only	
Birth weight	25-35 lbs.	
Adult weight	600-1100 lbs.	450-750 lbs.
Adult shoulder height	55-65 ins.	50-55 ins.
Maximum life span	12-14 yrs.	18-21 yrs.

Reproduction:

Bulls: Sexually mature at 1½ to 2½ years, but most breeding done by bulls 4 years old and older.

Cows: Up to 25 percent may breed as yearlings. Most cows do not conceive until 2½ years old.

Calves: One per birth is usual; twins occur rarely.

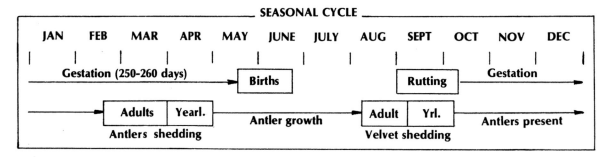

Food:

In summer the elk are primarily grazers, preferring blue grass, brome, wheatgrass, sedge, many forbs, mushrooms and horsetails. Winter fare is more opportunistic—browse of many shrubs and trees supplementing grasses that are revealed by pawing away snow.

Habitat:

Meadows, open prairie, parkland and forest.

Meadows and nearby woodlots become the elks' spring nursery.

By late summer the budding antlers have appeared and the bulls thrash the limbs to shed the itching casing.

Bull elk battle during the autumn rut.

A bull elk in summer displays his impressive velvet antler growth.

Migratory wintering elk herd, Waterton Lakes National Park.

Moose

Alces alces

Vital Statistics:

	Bull	Cow
Antlered sex	Bull only	
Birth weight	25-35 lbs.	
Adult weight	750-1200 lbs.	600-900 lbs.
Adult shoulder height	72-78 in.	68-74 in.
Maximum lifespan	15-20 yrs.	15-20 yrs.

Antlers:

Calves have flat, velvety knobs. Yearlings bear single spikes or small palms. Typical large palms occur after 4 or 5 years of age. Maximum spread about 5 feet.

Reproduction:

Bulls: Sexually mature as yearlings, but most breeding is by older bulls. Rutting period September-October.

Cows: Usually less than 20 percent conceive as yearlings, while 90 percent or more of older cows bear calves. Gestation period 240-250 days.

Calves: One is typical, particularly in young cows. Twinning rate usually 5 to 25 percent in older cows.

Food:

Mainly woody twigs (browse), and aquatic plants. Favorite browse includes willows, aspen, serviceberry, red-osier, dogwood, and alpine fir. Aquatic plants eaten include water crowfoot, hornwort, leafy pondweed, and cattail bullrush.

Habitat:

The moose prefers the lakeshore, alder swamps, aspen parklands and shrubby clearings but many females and young move up to subalpine meadows in summer.

Calf learning to walk.

Moose are seldom seen far from water, which provide them with their main food source.

Cow moose and twin calves in northern tundra.

Large meadows and ponds offer moose food and protection.

Mule Deer

Odocoileus hemionus

Vital Statistics:

	Buck	Doe
Antlered sex	Buck only	
Birth weight	8-10 lbs.	
Adult weight	150-350 lbs.	80-175 lbs.
Adult shoulder height	42 in.	40 in.
Maximum lifespan	15-20 yrs.	

Antlers:

Quite variable with age. Yearlings usually bear spikes or two points on each side. Most typical adult bucks have 5 to 7 points on each side.

Reproduction:

Bucks: Sexually mature as yearlings, but most breeding done by older bucks. Rutting period late October to early January.

Does: Most conceive as yearlings in their second autumn, and produce first fawn at two years of age. Gestation period about 7 months.

Fawns: Does usually have single fawn in first birth and twins thereafter. Triplets are rare. Birth period May-early June.

Food:

Mainly woody twigs (browse), but some grass taken in spring and herbs in summer. Bitterbrush, mountain mahogany, sagebrush, serviceberry, juniper, chokecherry, aspen and oak are favorite foods where available.

Habitat:

The mule deer prefers open coniferous forests, aspen parkland, steep broken terrain and shuns open prairie and thick dark coniferous forests.

A mule deer doe nurses her new born fawn.

A distinctive feature, which gives this deer its name, is its long, large ears, similar to that of a mule

White-Tailed Deer

Odocoileus virginanus

Vital Statistics:

	Buck	Doe
Antlered sex	Buck only	
Birth weight	7½ lbs.	6 lbs.
Adult weight	150-300 lbs.	110-160 lbs.
Adult shoulder height	36-40 in.	35-36 in.
Maximum lifespan	12-15 yrs.	15-18 yrs.

Antlers:

Yearlings usually produce spike or two-point antlers, but up to 8 points recorded. Typical adults have 5 to 8 points on each antler.

Reproduction:

Bucks: Sexually mature as yearlings, but most breeding done by older bucks. Rutting period October-November.

Does: Small percentage may breed as fawns, but most not until yearling age. Gestation period 205-210 days.

Fawns: Yearlings usually bear a single fawn. Twinning is frequent in older does, while triplets are rare.

Food:

Mainly woody twigs (browse), but some grass, herbs, fruits and mushrooms in spring and summer. Common foods include aspen, rose, chokecherry, serviceberry and willows.

Habitat:

Prefer open edges of deciduous forests, glades, stream banks and in grassland and prairie areas frequent wooded draws during day, and forage open prairie at twilight.

36

The white-tailed deer is the most familiar and abundant deer throughout most of North America.

White-tails prefer open woodlets and farm land and have entered the Rocky Mountain area through many of the river valleys. While the spotted fawns are difficult to differentiate from mule deer, the brown and white tail in adults lacks the black tip of the mule deer.

37

Pronghorn Antelope

Antilocapra

Vital Statistics:

	Buck	Doe
Horned sex	Buck and doe	
Birth weight	4-5 lbs.	
Adult weight	110-160 lbs.	100-130 lbs.
Adult shoulder height	33-36 in.	32-35 in.
Maximum lifespan	10-12 yrs.	

Horns:

Both sexes have black horns with a forward prong and curved tips. Buck horns up to 20 in. long; those of female much smaller and often lacking. Sheaths shed in late fall.

Reproduction:

Bucks: Sexually mature as yearlings, but most breeding done by older bucks. Rutting period September-October.

Does: Conception rarely occurs in first autumn . Most yearling and older does conceive annually. Gestation period 230-240 days.

Fawns: Twins are the rule, singles and triplets occurring less commonly. Season of birth April-June.

Food:

Browse plants make up over half of the annual diet. Those include sagebrush, rabbitbrush, and winter fat. Grasses are important in spring, and a variety of herbs in summer.

Habitat:

The pronghorns are animals of the open plains, steppes, and foothills, seeking protection in coulees and river valleys.

In summer pronghorn antelope feed on a variety of lush prairie grasses, and in winter they mainly browse on sagebrush.

The pronghorn antelope is the fastest land mammal in North America, able to attain speeds of up to 60 mph.

Black Bear

Ursus americanus

Vital Statistics:

Weight:

Birth	½ lb.
Cubs (6 months)	20-30 lb.
Yearlings	40-60 lb.
Adult females	100-225 lb.
Adult males	250-400 lb.

Size:

Female height at shoulder	2-3 ft.
Total length	5 ft.
Male height at shoulder	2½-3 ft.
Total length	6 ft.
Adult tracks	about 7″ long
Adult droppings	under 2″ diameter

Reproduction:

One to four cubs are born in the den during late January or early February. Cubs weigh less than half a pound at birth, are weaned at five months, but don't become independent until after the first winter's denning with their mother. The sow chases the yearling cubs away before mating again. Therefore productive sows only breed every two years. Maturity is reached at 4-5 years.

Food:

Black bears are omnivorous—eating vegetation and animal matter with the latter being either freshly caught or more commonly rotting carrion. In spring after emerging from the winter den, they eat conifer needles and new grass shoots and seek out horsetails and berries as the season progresses. Garbage dumps are favorite feasting areas.

Habitat:

Blacks inhabit both coniferous and deciduous forests and associated openings from sea level to subalpine areas. Caves or hollows under stumps are favored denning sites which are occupied from October-December through to April.

Black bear feeding on spawned salmon carcass.

The black bear is one of the main wildlife attractions at mountain national parks. They can be viewed from the safety of a vehicle along roadsides during the early summer.

The black bear exists in several other color phases including brown, blond, and cinnamon, with a white blaze on chest.

Although black bears are the smallest of all North American bears, they have very strong protective instincts over their cubs.

Grizzly Bear

Ursus arctos

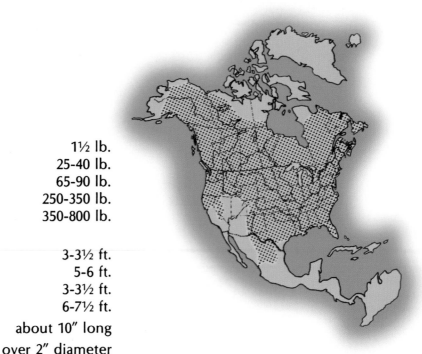

Vital Statistics:

Weight:

Weight at birth	1½ lb.
Weight of cubs (6 months)	25-40 lb.
Weight of yearlings	65-90 lb.
Weight of adult females	250-350 lb.
Weight of adult males	350-800 lb.

Size:

Female height at shoulder	3-3½ ft.
Total length	5-6 ft.
Male height at shoulder	3-3½ ft.
Total length	6-7½ ft.
Adult tracks	about 10" long
Adult droppings	over 2" diameter

Reproduction:

Like the black bear, and most other mammals for that matter, grizzly sows cannot conceive while lactating so generally only have cubs every second year. Sexual maturity is attained at 6 years. The average litter size is 2 but 1-4 is the range.

Food:

Grizzlies are omnivorous but predominately eat vegetation—succulent grasses, skunk cabbage, licorice root, etc. Ground squirrels and marmots are occasionally dug from their burrows and spawning salmon are priority foods when and where available. Winter and road kills are also utilized along with human garbage.

Habitat:

While preferring open areas, the grizzly has been so reduced in numbers that it has been pushed into areas remote from man. These are largely alpine and subalpine meadows of the mountain parks or wilderness areas. After emerging from the winter den, lower areas are first to yield succulent vegetation. Winter dens are dug rather than natural hollows as used by the black bears.

Grizzly sow and her cubs snooze during midday along the Arctic shoreline.

44

During mating season, male grizzlies will occasionally engage in ferocious battle.

Grizzly bears will gorge themselves during berry season to fatten up for winter hibernation.

A bold grizzly bear approaches a bull moose.

Mountain grizzlies seek spring shoots and dandelions.

A pair of grizzlies argue over a fishing spot.

46

Young grizzly cub frolicking.

Grizzly cub and sow feeding on blueberries on the Alaska tundra.

Cougar
Felis concolor

Vital Statistics:

Weight (pounds):

At birth	1
Adult male	160 (125 - 200)
Adult female	100 (80 - 135)

Total length:

Adult male	6½ - 9 ft.
Adult female	6 - 7 ft.

Shoulder height:

Adult male	26 - 32 in.
Adult female	22 - 28 in.

Reproduction:

Cougars can mate and subsequently give birth at any season but most young seem to be born in January and February. One to five kittens, with three being the average, are born after a 90 day gestation period. The young become independent at one and one-third to two years and reach sexual maturity at two to three years.

Food:

The cougar primarily feeds upon mammals: deer being the staple diet 77%, porcupine 9%, domestic animals 4%, beaver 4%, horses 2%, with miscellaneous mammals (sheep, goats, elk, moose, lynx and mice, etc.) and grasses rounding out its meals. Kills are often covered with leaves and provide several meals. Cougars hunt during daylight but become most active at dawn and dusk.

Habitat:

This wide ranging animal can effectively live from sea level to the alpine zone and from thick forests to open grassland. However, it now largely resides in the wild mountainous terrain of the Rockies westward.

Cougars remain solitary, except during mating season.

48

Young cougar
kittens out of
their den
during early
spring.

Cougars are very efficient hunters and prefer deer as their main prey.

Young cougars may remain with their mother for as long as two years before surviving on their own.

Cougars are
very strong
swimmers.

Bobcat

Lynx rufus

Vital Statistics:

Weight (pounds):
At birth	½
Adult male	21 (20 - 35)
Adult female	15 (12 - 25)

Total length:
Adult male	34 in. (30 - 37)
Adult female	32 in. (30 - 35)

Reproduction:

Mating occurs between February and June with one to seven young (average of three) being born from May to July after a 50 to 65 day gestation period. The young become independent at six to eight months and reach maturity at one year.

Food:

Nearly half the bobcat's fare is made up of hares and cottontails, one-quarter rats and mice and the balance an assortment of small mammals, birds, reptiles and insects, though occasionally small deer are captured.

Habitat:

More versatile than its northern cousin, the bobcat fares well from forest to open, dry, rocky hills or even the outskirts of cities.

Despite its size, the bobcat can be a very aggressive little hunter, taking down animals much larger than itself.

To the observer a bobcat resembles a large version of the house cat.

Lynx

Lynx lynx

Vital Statistics:

Weight (pounds):
At birth	½
Adult male	24 (15 - 35)
Adult female	20 (12 - 26)

Total length:
Adult male	35 in. (30 - 42)
Adult female	33 in. (30 - 38)

Reproduction:

Lynx populations fluctuate greatly around the 10 year varying hare cycle. The peak and crash of the lynx population follows about one year behind that of its main food source, the hare. The one to six (average two to three) young are born in May to June, become independent by six to eight months, and mature at one year of age.

Food:

The lynx is a nocturnal hunter, preying primarily upon varying hares, grouse, mice and carrion. In the "crash" years of the hares, lynx often disperse southward from their northern boreal forest wilderness and in a desperate search for food frequently get into trouble with chicken farmers.

Habitat:

The lynx is primarily a forest dweller.

With wide and heavily furred paws, lynx are able to move silently and swiftly through deep snow in pursuit of prey.

A young lynx kitten.

Wolf
Canis lupus

Vital Statistics:

Weight (pounds):

At birth	1½ - 2
Adult male	100 (80 - 175)
Adult female	85 (65 - 130)

Total length:

Adult male	65 - 73 in.
Adult female	58 - 65 in.

Shoulder height:

Adult male	30 - 38 in.
Adult female	26 - 34 in.

Food:

The wolf is primarily a hunter of big game: deer, elk, moose, sheep and caribou being the staple species where abundant. Smaller mammals and birds are also important. Quantitative studies have shown the wolves primarily prey upon the young, aged or sick animals.

Habitat:

Wolves inhabit every niche from open plains to deep forest.

Reproduction:

Wolves presumably mate for life. Peak mating occurs during the two weeks around the beginning of March, with pupping peaking 60 to 63 days later. More than a dozen pups in a litter have been recorded, but seven is average. Pups start to join in on hunting expeditions by September. Females are mature at two while males mature at three years of age.

The wolf is perhaps North America's least loved predator. Exterminated over most of the continent, its strongholds remain in the Arctic northern forest, and scattered parks along British Columbia's coasts with a few bastions in the Canadian parks.

Gray wolves feeding on a kill.

Although wolves prefer large animals, they will also hunt for smaller mammals such as hares and rodents.

Gray wolf family rest near their den site.

Wolf fur colors vary from white to black to the more common gray.

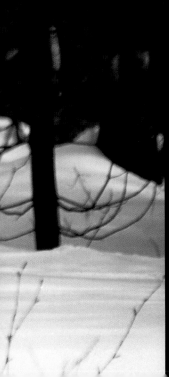

Gray wolf on the northern tundra.

Coyote

Canis latrans

Vital Statistics:

Weight (pounds):

At birth	½
Adult male	35
Adult female	23

Total length:

Adult male	45 - 73 in.
Adult female	42 - 47 in.

Food:

About one-third of the diet is made up of hares and cottontail rabbits and another one-third of carrion. The balance is a wide variety of small mammals, birds, insects, etc., with mice being dominant, though poultry plays an important role with some individuals.

Habitat:

The versatile coyote prefers open forests and grasslands and can be found from valley bottoms to alpine tundra.

Reproduction:

The coyote is only sexually active from late January to late March and after a gestation of 60 to 63 days gives birth to three to ten young (average six). The young become self-sufficient at six to nine months but don't become sexually mature until one and one-half to two years.

Coyotes can become well adapted to a variety of habitats.

Coyote pups playing. Coyotes have been known to have up to 19 young in a litter but five to seven pups are most common.

The coyote is omnivorous, either catching prey, scrounging carrion or seeking out vegetation. Cottontails, snowshoe hares and small rodents constitute most of his prey. Through pack cooperation they can occasionally kill deer, antelope and sheep.

Red Fox
Vulpes vulpes

Vital Statistics:

Weight (pounds):

At birth	¼
Adult male	10 (9 - 15)
Adult female	8 (7 - 10)

Total length:

Adult male	40 - 46 in.
Adult female	36 - 42 in.

Food:

The red fox is omnivorous with a strong preference for meats. These are primarily small mammals: mice, ground squirrels, moles, muskrats, cottontails and hares. An assortment of birds, insects and a very wide variety of vegetation, including berries, corn, grasses, apples, etc., make up its fare.

Habitat:

Red foxes prefer the forest openings and edges and along lakeshores or streambeds.

Reproduction:

The three to ten young are born from March to May after a 49 to 53 day gestation period. The pups appear above ground at one month, become independent at 15 weeks and become sexually mature at one year.

The young pups are weaned at one month and start to play around the den entrance. Home life is short and by four months of age they abandon the family unit to fend for themselves. The young are mature at ten months.

Long-Tailed Weasel
Mustela frenata

Vital Statistics:

Weight:
Females   3 - 4 oz.
Males   6 - 9 oz.

Length:
Females   16 in.
Males   18 in.

Reproduction:

Breeding season   July - August
Birth season   March to May
Gestation period   220 - 337 days
Litter size   6 (3 - 9)

Food:

This little weasel primarily feeds upon meadow voles, deer mice, chipmunks, pocket gophers, ground squirrels and prairie dogs though any small vertebrate or invertebrate will be taken. Little vegetation is consumed.

Habitat:

The long-tailed weasel frequents waterways in open grassland, parklands and the open alpine meadows.

The fur of the long-tailed weasel turns white in the winter, except for the black tip on its tail.

66

Marten

Martes americana

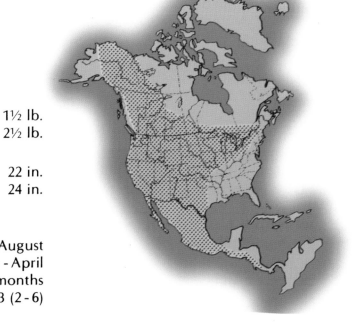

Vital Statistics:

Weight:	
Females	1½ lb.
Males	2½ lb.
Length:	
Females	22 in.
Males	24 in.

Reproduction:

Breeding season	July - August
Birth season	March - April
Gestation period	8½ - 9 months
Litter size	3 (2 - 6)

Food:

Mice (65%) and squirrels (10%) are the staple food though any small animal is potential food. Considerable berries are eaten during the summer.

Habitat:

This specialist is restricted to the climax (mature and long standing) coniferous forest.

Wolverine

Gulo gulo

Vital Statistics:

Weight:
Females	22 lb.
Males	32 lb.

Length:
Females	35 in.
Males	40 in.

Reproduction:

Breeding season	May - June
Birth season	February - April
Gestation period	7 - 8 months
Litter size	2.5 (1.5)

Food:

The wolverine is primarily a scavenger living on winter kills and prey caught by wolves, lynx or bears. They also capture deer—it is believed by dropping onto them from trees. A wide range of vegetation is also consumed along with a variety of smaller mammals (beaver, mice, porcupine, etc.), birds and even fish.

Habitat:

The wolverine is a mammal of the boreal forest and subalpine to alpine zones but also follows herds of caribou out onto the tundra.

Pound for pound the wolverine is known as one of the most powerful and ferocious predators in North America.

68

River Otter

Lontra canadensis

Vital Statistics:

Weight:
Female	16 lb.
Male	18 lb.

Length:
Female	44 in.
Male	46 in.

Reproduction:

Breeding season	February - March
Birth season	March - April
Gestation period	9½ - 12½ months
Litter size	3 (1 - 5)

Food:

The river or land otter specializes in catching its food underwater. Inland over 90% of this is fish: minnows, sunfish, catfish, sculpins, perch and trout. Invertebrates, amphibians and even muskrats or birds will be taken. On the seacoast many additional marine invertebrates are consumed.

Habitat:

Riparian to the extreme, the otter is seldom found away from a waterway whether at sea level or in an alpine glacial pool.

Mink

Mustela vision

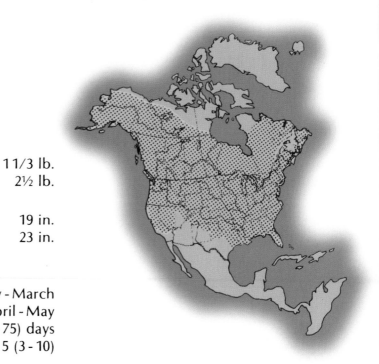

Vital Statistics:

Weight:

Females	1 1/3 lb.
Males	2½ lb.

Length:

Females	19 in.
Males	23 in.

Reproduction:

Breeding season	February - March
Birth season	April - May
Gestation period	50 (40 - 75) days
Litter size	5 (3 - 10)

Food:

Small mammals and fish make up about one-third of the mink's diet with amphibians, reptiles, birds, insects and worms filling out this active predator's prey. In some areas the muskrats form the major item, in others it might be voles. Minnows, dace and shiners are the favored fish species.

Habitat:

Mink are riparian, frequenting the forest edges of streams, rivers, ponds, lakes and seashore.

A mink hunting along the banks of an icy stream in early spring.

70

Badger

Taxidea taxus

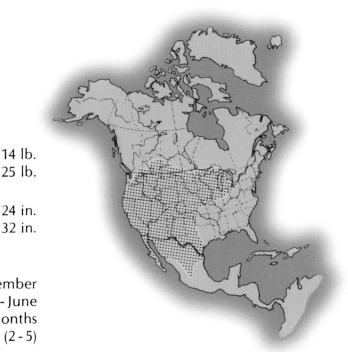

Vital Statistics:

Weight:
Females	14 lb.
Males	25 lb.

Length:
Females	24 in.
Males	32 in.

Reproduction:

Breeding season	August - September
Birth season	May - June
Gestation period	7 - 9 months
Litter size	3 (2 - 5)

Food:

The badger is largely a specialized feeder—its large claws being adapted for digging small mammals out of their burrows. Ground squirrels, pocket gophers, prairie dogs and other small rodents are the prime prey though ground nesting birds, eggs, and many insects and reptiles are eaten as well.

Habitat:

Badgers live in open country or in clearings in dryer areas.

Badgers are nocturnal hunters.

Striped Skunk

Mephitis mephitis

Vital Statistics:

Weight:
Female	3 lb.
Male	4 lb.

Length:
Female	22 in.
Male	23 in.

Reproduction:

Breeding season	February - March
Birth season	May
Gestation period	63 days
Litter size	5 (2 - 10)

Food:

The skunk is a true omnivore, opportunistically feeding upon whatever is available, whether it be carrion, birds' eggs, insects, small mammals, grasses or succulent berries or frogs and fish.

Habitat:

The striped skunk prefers well hedged agricultural land or open forests and river bottoms.

With tail arched, this striped skunk displays a behavior which first serves as a warning of its intention to spray.

Pika

Ochotona princeps

Vital Statistics:

Average weight (adult)	5 - 9 oz.
Average length (adult)	7 - 8 in.
Winter color	gray - brown

Reproduction:

Breeding age of females	1 year
Litters per year	2
Litter size	3 (1 - 6)
Gestation period (days)	30
Breeding season	April - July

Food:

In the restricted alpine environment almost every plant is eaten, with grasses, sedges, lupines, paintbrush and willows being but a few. These grasses are sun dried to cure them and then stored underground in chambers, sometimes surrounded by ice, to be eaten throughout winter as the pika does not hibernate.

Habitat:

Pikas live in talus slopes and in rock piles usually above timberline in the alpine zone but occasionally into the forested areas if there is sufficient rocky habitat. In winter they are active below the snow cover in the rock piles.

A pika gathers up its food cache to store in haystacks.

Snowshoe Hare

Lepus americanus

Vital Statistics:

Average weight (adult)	2.5 - 4.0 lb.
Average length (adult)	17 - 19 in.
Winter color	white

Reproduction:

Breeding age of females	1 yr.
Litters per year	3 - 4
Litter size	3.5 (2-7)
Gestation period (days)	36 - 37
Breeding season	March - August

Food:

In summer succulent grasses and many herbs are eaten along with leaves of trembling aspen, birch and willow. In winter their fare is the buds, twigs and branches of many shrubs and trees. As the snow deepens they can reach higher and higher by standing on the frozen crust.

Habitat:

This hare prefers the thickets and heavy coniferous and deciduous forests from which it works outward for feeding in the more open areas.

The snowshoe hare turns white in the winter and brown in the summer to blend in with its environment.

White Tailed Jack Rabbit
Lepus towndendii

Vital Statistics:

Average weight (adult)	6.5 - 12 lb.
Average length (adult)	20 - 26 in.
Winter color	white

Reproduction:

Breeding age of females	1 yr.
Litters per year	3 - 4
Litter size	5 (1 - 9)
Gestation period (days)	28 - 30
Breeding season	March - July

Food:

Grasses and clover are favored summer fare with buds and the bark of trees and shrubs forming most of the winter food.

Habitat:

White-tailed jack rabbits favor the open sagebrush plains and pasture land and only seek shelter during blizzars in forest cover. In the mountainous areas they will penetrate the open pine-juniper forests.

Instead of walking or running, jack rabbits will normally hop in five- to ten-foot leaps.

Hoary Marmot
Marmota caligata

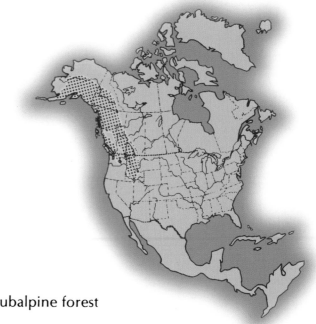

Vital Statistics:

Average adult:
  Length:
    Male   30 in.
    Female   28 in.
Weight   10 - 20 lb.

Reproduction:

Litter size   3 - 5

Habitat:

Boulder strewn alpine slopes and rocky openings in subalpine forest

Hoary marmots live in colonies in the high mountain alpine slopes.

During the summer marmots fatten up on lush alpine plants, for they spend over six months in hibernation.

Yellow Bellied Marmot

Marmota flaviventris

Vital Statistics:

Average adult:
  Length:

Male	22 in.
Female	20 in.
Weight	7 - 12 lb.

Reproduction:

Litter size	3 - 8

Habitat:

Dry, rocky valleys and slopes in the north, but extends into alpine zone from Wyoming southward.

Woodchuck

Marmota monax

Vital Statistics:

Average adult:
Length	16 - 24 in.
Weight	5 - 7 lb.

Reproduction:

Gestation period	31 - 32 days
Litter size	3.5 (1 - 8)

Habitat:

Open woodlots, pastures and fence rows, particularly where buildings and stumps occur. This animal has greatly benefitted from agricultural practices which have opened up the land.

Richardson's Ground Squirrel

Spermophilus richardsonii

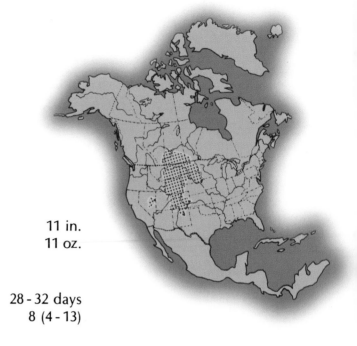

Vital Statistics:

Average adult:
Length	11 in.
Weight	11 oz.

Reproduction:

Gestation period	28 - 32 days
Litter size	8 (4 - 13)

Habitat:

Sage plains and grasslands from 5,000 ft. to above timberline. Also openings in montane forest in Wyoming and Colorado.

A Richardson's ground squirrel gathers up nesting material.

More commonly called gophers, these ground squirrels become well adapted in areas of human populations.

Columbian Ground Squirrel

Spermophilus columbianus

Vital Statistics:

Average adult:
Length	14 in.
Weight	17 oz.

Reproduction:
Gestation period	24 days
Litter size	3.5 (2 - 7)

Habitat:

Meadows, forest openings and alpine parks. Usually colonial.

As a hibernator for almost 70% of the year like many other squirrels, male Columbian ground squirrels are the first to appear in spring.

Thirteen Lined Ground Squirrel

Spermophilus tridecemlineatus

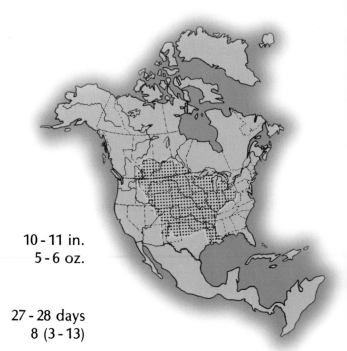

Vital Statistics:

Average adult:
Length   10 - 11 in.
Weight   5 - 6 oz.

Reproduction:

Gestation period   27 - 28 days
Litter size   8 (3 - 13)

Habitat:

Parklands, abandoned, overgrown fields, but not open grassland.

This ground squirrel will construct its burrow from fifteen to twenty feet long, sometimes even longer.

Golden Mantled Ground Squirrel

Spermophilus lateralis

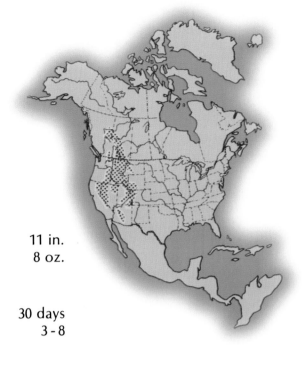

Vital Statistics:

Average adult:
Length	11 in.
Weight	8 oz.

Reproduction:
Gestation period	30 days
Litter size	3 - 8

Habitat:

Open woodland, in rocky situations, lower slopes to alpine zone.

The golden-mantled ground squirrel can often be seen carrying food in its well-developed cheek pouches.

Flying Squirrel
Glaucomys sabrinus

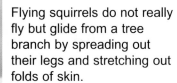

Vital Statistics:

Average adult:
Length	12½ in.
Weight	5 - 6 oz.

Reproduction:
Gestation period	37-40 days
Litter size	3 - 6

Habitat:

Well forested mountain slopes with fairly mature tree growth.

Flying squirrels do not really fly but glide from a tree branch by spreading out their legs and stretching out folds of skin.

Red Spruce Squirrel

Tamiasciurus hudsonicus

Vital Statistics:

Average adult:
Length	13 in.
Weight	8½ - 9 oz.

Reproduction:

Gestation period	36 - 40 days
Litter size	4 (1 - 8)

Habitat:

Fairly dense coniferous forests of the montane and subalpine zones.

The red squirrel is active throughout the whole year.

In autumn the red squirrel will bury its food cache containing mostly green pine cones and seeds.

Yellow Pine Chipmunk

Eutamias amoenus

Vital Statistics:

Average adult:
Length	8½ in
Weight	2½ oz.

Reproduction:

Litter size	4 - 8

Habitat:

Primarily parklands, dry montane forests and lower subalpine zone.

During the summer this tiny but inquisitive chipmunk will often visit occupied campsites searching for food scraps.

Porcupine

Erethizon dorsatum

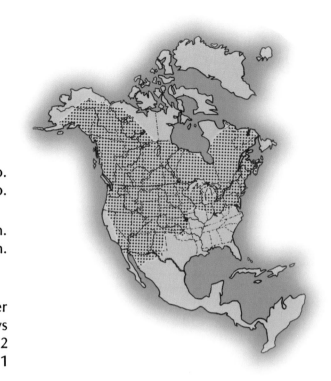

Vital Statistics:

Weight:
Adult male	18 - 25 lb.
Adult female	15 - 23 lb.

Total length:
Adult male	33 in.
Adult female	30 in.

Reproduction:

Mating season	late fall-winter
Gestation period	110 - 120 days
Litter size	1 - 2
Litters per year	1

Food:

The porcupine is a vegetarian, primarily living during summer on the leaves of many shrubs and trees or on grasses, pond lily or even corn. In winter it feeds upon the highly nutritive cambium layer of a variety of coniferous and deciduous trees. Antlers, road signs and human implements are chewed for their mineral and salt content.

Habitat:

The porcupine primarily inhabits the forest, either coniferous or deciduous, but will venture out into open grassland during summer.

The porcupine is strictly vegetarian and is mainly active at night.

A porcupine's body, excluding its underparts, is armed with several thousand sharp quills.

Beaver

Castor canadensis

Vital Statistics:

Weight:
Adult male	25 - 55 lb.
Adult female	25 - 55 lb.

Total length:
Adult male	38 (36 - 43) in.
Adult female	36 (34 - 40) in.

Reproduction:

Mating season	winter
Gestation period	90 - 110 days
Litter size	3 (1 - 7)
Age at first reproduction	2 yrs.
Litter per year	1

Food:

In summer, pond succulents such as water-lillies, cattails, and duckweed, are the main fare supplemented with leaves, buds and some bark of trees. In winter the highly nutritious cambium layer become the staple food. Trembling aspen is favored but a variety of trees are consumed. These include willows, birch, cottonwood, poplar, and occasionally pine and spruce. It is estimated that one acre of aspen will keep one beaver one year. Food is eaten underwater or in the hut.

Habitat:

Beavers inhabit lakes, ponds and slow moving streams that are surrounded by trees.

The beaver has large incisor teeth, which continue to grow throughout the animal's lifetime, are also used for carrying branches.

Muskrat
Ondatra zibethicus

Vital Statistics:

Weight:
adult   Adult 2 - 3 lb.

Total length:
Adult   24 in.

Reproduction:

Mating season	spring through fall
Gestation period	25 - 30 days
Litter size	1 - 11
Age at first reproduction	6 months
Litters per year	2 - 6

Food:

Summer food is mainly emergent vegetation such as bulrushes, cattails, sedge and water lilies, while winter food is mainly submerged vegetation (so it isn't frozen) such as water lily tubers, bladderwort, etc. Fresh-water mussels, frogs, salamanders and even catfish are consumed.

Habitat:

Muskrats live in slow moving water that does not freeze over in winter.

A muskrat brings a food supply to its feeding platform.

Rocky Mountain Birds - Raptors

The bald eagle was first declared an endangered species in 1973 but, after significant conservation efforts, it was reclassified as a threatened species in 1996 and is now locally abundant in the Northwest.

The golden eagle is usually restricted to mountainous regions, where it has been known to fly into bighorn sheep and knock them off cliff sides as a hunting technique.

Bald eagles are enormous birds. Their wings span more than six feet (two meters). Bald eagles live over thirty years. Their nest is the largest of any bird in North America. They can see six or seven times farther than people, and use their massive talons and beaks to kill and handle prey.

Swainson's Hawk makes the second longest migration of any raptor species, and is somewhat unique among the hawk family in that outside of the breeding season, the main part of its diet consists of insects.

Peregrine falcons are renowned for their incredible speed, exceeding 180 mph when pursuing prey. They hit their prey with their breastbone rather than their feet, which would shatter at such speeds.

Male ruffed grouse will often be heard 'drumming' from their log during the breeding season, and on occasion have been known to attack the feet of observers.

Male sage grouse will congregate during the breeding season to form their display 'lek' which can usually be seen from the road. Females will observe each male and choose the one of their liking.

Rocky Mountain Birds - Various Species

The yellow-headed blackbird is often seen in marshlands, from the interior regions of British Columbia, south to New Mexico.

Sandhill Cranes are the most abundant crane species on the planet, and are commonly seen in the Northwest region during the winter.

Two male sharp-tailed grouse performing their breeding display in the interior of BC.

The eldest sandhill chick will often out-compete the younger one, which will lead to its eventual death in most clutches.

Sharp-tailed grouse are fairly common in grassland and sagebrush areas of the interior regions of the Pacific Northwest and similar to the sage-grouse, males will be seen to 'lek' on the spring breeding grounds.

Like all Corvids, magpies are very inventive and resourceful birds, and are considered pests on many farms as they find ingenious ways to get into feed supplies.

The downy woodpecker is the most common woodpecker in North America and is often confused with the hairy woodpecker, which is larger in size and has a larger bill. Both are often seen at suet feeders in the winter.

Ravens are often heard before they are seen, and they can be heard from quite distance. They are often associated with camp grounds and other areas where visitors offer them food.

A female spruce grouse with a chick. Spruce grouse are commonly referred to as 'fool hens' due to the their willingness to remain stationary upon close approach.

The gray jay or whisky-jack is a very common resident in the boreal forests of North America. They are remarkably tame and will often eat from the hand if offered food.

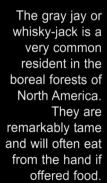

The ghostly call of the common loon is often heard in the interior regions of the Pacific Northwest.